Penny & Me

Maria Teresa Ornelas Ibarra

Illustrated by Jake Johnson

Penny & Me

ISBN: 978-0-578-90906-6

Published by Espibano
Printed and bound in the United States of America

Dedicated to Carmen Dimas Acosta
"Penny"

Contents

New Kids on the Block

It began one summer day in 1968. A car pulling a moving van drove up across the street from my house on Third Street, which was next to an empty house with the police station and library across from it to the west. We watched attentively as they began stepping out of the car, first, a tall, slender, man got out of the car, then a shorter woman with short black hair, she was a nice looking woman in her late thirties. Then came the kids, a skinny boy, a tall, thin, gangly, looking girl with long, black, straight hair, and a younger girl with short, black hair. My brothers, Billy, Bobby, Rudy, Eddie, and I were sitting outside in our front yard on the cement steps watching these new people as they unloaded their van.

Bobby, being humorous, said, "That one (speaking of the boy), looks like a real pansy," making various sounds to describe him. Then we noticed the braces on the younger girl's legs, and we felt bad for her and wondered why she had to wear them. My mom (Esperanza) and dad (Urbano) were watching us, my dad was sitting by the table near the window, put down the book he was reading to come to the door, my mom also left her cooking to come to the door. They reminded us that staring at people is not nice, and we should mind our own business anyway.

They then told us that we could introduce ourselves when the time was right, and that maybe we could also offer them some help. Then they went back to what they had been doing. Billy, Bobby, and I decided we'd wait to introduce ourselves till later, though at the mature ages of 10, 11, and 13, to us, the right time was unpredictable. It could have been at any minute, or any second, as far as we were concerned. But our parents had already given us explicit instructions not to bother anybody, so we picked up the football and headed to the street.

While we were passing the ball around, our four-year-old curly, haired sister Anita came running out of the house with curls flying about her, yelling, "Did you see the people that are moving in over there? Do you know their names yet?"

"Shut up!" we all hollered. Bobby decided to make her go inside and tossed the ball at her, so she ran inside the house to tell on us, as she usually did. We continued playing as though nothing had happened.

Several days went by. The family had settled in and we hadn't become acquainted yet. It was summer, as long as we had our chores done, we were allowed to do whatever we wanted, which was normally to be outside playing something, most of the time it was football. One day while we were enjoying a game of football, we noticed the three kids sitting on their porch watching us, as they had done a few other times.

Billy decided it was time for an introduction. He walked over to them and said, "Hi, do you want to play with us?" All three looked up at him with excitement on their faces.

They looked at one another, and the boy said, "We don't know how to play." Billy then said, "That's OK. We don't play that well anyway. We'll show you how to play." The boy and older girl stood up, but the younger girl with braces remained sitting. She said, "I can't play my mom won't let me," so she watched us play. As Billy came to the middle of the street he introduced himself and us. The boy's name was Tommy, and the older girl was named Penny, her real name was Carmen, and the younger girl was named Charlene, called Mimee.

As we were playing, we noticed they were right, they didn't know how to play. They were clumsy and awkward. I thought to myself, "How are we going to act around them, they really are pansies. Little did I know that Penny was going to end up being my best friend, and so to speak, my partner in crime.

Better Acquainted

As time went by, and once we became better acquainted, which didn't take too long, we got along well. We didn't mind that they were clumsy and awkward, and they didn't mind us giving some instruction. Frankly, they were will to earn and they were really getting pretty good in sports. They were pretty intelligent, also. Although Mimee was still very limited on what she was allowed to do, we would break some of her mother's rule and sneak her into our games. Football wasn't all we knew how to play, we also flew kites, rode bikes played baseball, went swimming, fish, and played games like freeze tag, four corners, and a game called "los lostinos."

Many of these games were easy for Mimee to join in, plus we would come to find out that this was good for her physically and emotionally. Every day was a new experience for them and us. We shared every piece of equipment necessary for whatever activity was going on. We had so much fun. There was nothing more we needed than each other's company to pass the time away. Soon Penny and I were each known as being "one of the guys" because we were such tomboys. You would know it to look at us; we were no raving beauties. We had scraped knees, our hair was normally in braids, we wore boys' tennies, we like playing in dirt, and we also liked picking up and abusing poor, tiny insects. It was not likely for us to have clean pockets. We kept everything in them, including those tiny animals with no life left in them. We did carry around a ball and some jax. We were pretty good at playing that. We even had jax contest, our brothers included. Surprisingly, they were good at playing jax also.

We were capable of doing a few girls things, especially since my dad, brothers, and older sisters kept reminding us that we were girls. They used to sit us down and talk to us about how girls should act and dress. My sisters, Romelia, Dolores, and Josie dared us to comb our hair like girls with curls, and such. We sort of liked it, but we wouldn't admit it.

They went as far as buying and "Easy Curl" hair setter for young girls to help us learn how to maintain our hair, simply, just so that we would do something decent o our messy hair. However, bows were totally out of the question! Penny and I like wearing bracelets, and plenty of them. One day, my sister Dolores told us that we were weird because we were such tomboys, yet we like wearing bracelets. She said we worried her. We had no idea why, so we kept being our "weird" selves. We carried on as usual, we would listen to what everyone would have to say, tried to please them, so we'd some-times play with a Barbie doll, make sock dresses for them, we'd even try to comb our hair nicely once in a while. We even tried the "Easy Curl," some lipstick, eyeliner, and mascara. It was a sight to Not Behold. Nobody said anything to us, they simply looked at us and looked away, or put their heads down. I do recall my dad making a slight grunting sound when he saw us. There was never a dull moment in our youthful lives.

A Nonshocking Experience

We awoke early to the same things we normally did: cleaning, washing, etc. I worked weekends and got home around one in the afternoon. When I arrived home, Penny would come over. My mom always seemed to know the exact time of her arrival. What she couldn't predict was when she would be going home. Sometimes we would all play outside pretty late. My parents were normally sitting on the porch keeping an eye on us. Other times we just did some fun things inside or in the back yard. Many times, my mom would want us to go to bed early, so she would call us all in. She would then tell our friends that it was time to go home because it was getting late. Tommy, Mimmee, and whatever other friends were there at the time would usually leave. Penny would usually agree, but then we just continue with whatever we were doing. So my mom would again remind Penny it was time to go.

"Good night," she would say to her.

Penny would look at her and respond, "Good night Mrs. Ornelas, sweet dreams."

My mom soon came to realize that this girl was pretty close to a permanent fixture in our home. I don't know if my mom did it just for laughs or what, but she seemed to have that ritual with Penny quite often. Penny never meant any disrespect, it was only that we were usually enjoying ourselves.

My Dad worked graveyard with the Southern Pacific as a machinist and my mom would pack hi a lunch before he left. We often had the opportunity to take his lunch to him. We were usually lucky enough she would make enough for all of us. Those bean and cheese burritos on homemade tortillas were also a good reason for Penny to stick around. It's a wonder we didn't gain so much wright with the things we ate, most of the time in the evening. The times we would take my dad his lunch, we would sit and watch him work for a while, then he'd realize we were there, and he would greet us. Sometimes he would let us have some of his lunch. For us, watching him work was a real treat.

One hot, summer day we decided to go swimming as soon as I got home from work. There was only one problem" we had no money to pay with. So we decided to have a lemonade and cookie stand. We baked cookies and made lemonade at my house. Naturally, we made a mess, but we cleaned it up afterwards. When we were all set, we place our stand next door in the corner where the empty house was, where everyone could see us. At first, no one was buying anything from us, and, as usual, our brothers made fun of us. We were getting very disappointed.

My dad knew what we were doing, so he went to the depot and the Blue Moon Bar to let his co-workers and friends know about our stand. He made sure they came over. I don't know exactly how he did it, but he got them there. We suddenly had several customers. Our stand was a success, we were so happy! We not only made enough money to go swimming, which we weren't able to do until two days later because we didn't have much time left over in the day to go swimming, and because, the day after our great success, it rained. We then chose to go to the movies that night and buy ourselves goodies. Since it rained on the day that we had planned to go swimming, we stayed indoors and listened to music and danced. Well. I danced Penny had no rhythm, though she did try, and she did rather well. It was alright, we just enjoyed our ways of entertainment. We would once in a while get a, "turn down that music, and stop screaming." We would wonder why they said that when in fact we weren't screaming, we were singing.

With as many as there were in my family, we (all the kids) normally ended up in one of the rooms we shared. Rudy, Eddie, Mimmee, and Anita were there while we were singing and dancing. They imitated us—in a teasing manner, of course—but we didn't care, we continued on. We then noticed the rain had slowed down, so we fled outside to play boats. We would pick out the best sticks we could find, no bigger than four to five inches long, the, place them on the water that flowed alongside the curb, and race them against one another. We played boats until we became tired, or start arguing about one thing or another.

Penny and I were either daring or really nuts, because we liked walking while it was still sprinkling and/or during a thunder and lightning storm. After out boat competition we walked to the Cask and Carry store against our parents' advice.

We strolled along usually gabbing away, sometimes singing a few songs. It began to sprinkle harder as well as thunder and lightning. We continued to walk and came close to the electric power lines above us, we would stop and wait for it to thunder, and lightning, and we would run across the lines as quickly as we could so that we wouldn't be shocked by the lightning. We normally did this all the way to the store and all the way back home, but on this day, Mother Nature had a surprise for us. The water felt good as it softly landed on us, and we were enjoying catching the raindrops with our mouths. All of a sudden—BOOM, CRACK, POW! It seemed that the lightning had struck one of the electric poles. It felt as though the earth had shaken beneath us! We let out a terrified scream, and held on to one another until we felt safe enough to let. We then ran into the store wet, and scared. The looks on our faces must have given the lady working reason enough to ask if we were alright. We answered, "Si Senora (yes ma'am)," then bought a couple of two-for-a-nickel cinnamon suckers. We gave our thanks to the lady, started walking out the door, and she said, "Be careful girls."

We stopped and looked at each other under the safety of the little porch of the store; we were scared.

"OK," said Penny, let's wait for the lightning to strike, then let's run as fast as we can, all right?" I quickly agreed. We ran all the way home with only a few words to one another. It was such a bad storm with its loud thunder and lightning striking just about every few steps we ran. We ran, and ran as fast as we could, not paying attention to the things we usually paid attention to, including the water puddles, mud, and barking dogs. One of the dogs we forgot about ran right up to the top of the fence and barked and growled at us. Talk about double fear, there it was! We ran even faster tripping over each other, and our own feet a few times. Luckily we didn't fall.

When we got home we were soaked down to the bone, and shivering from fear. We entered the house from my room to avoid my parents. My dad noticed us and called us. We looked at each other, and our wet candy bag. I answered, "Mande, ("yes sir") I responded as I put the candy bag down on the floor behind the door.

"Where have you been?" he asked.

"Nowhere daddy we were sitting out in the garage waiting for the rain to slow down.

He gave us an "I don't believe you" look with a grin and walked into the living room, told us to change from those wet clothes. "How your clothes got so wet from here to the garage is beyond me," he said, then went on reading his Louis L'Amour book. We both gave a sigh of relief

Penny decided not to go home until her clothes were dry, so I changed and gave her something to change into. We hung our clothes in the bathroom and went back to my room to see the damage to our candy. It was OK, we sat on my bed looking out the window and began giggling about what we had just experienced. Eating our candy, looking at the rain, and counting the vehicles that went by. How dumb could we be: I do believe we were aware of lightning striking anywhere, and how dangerous it was for us to do what we had been doing though the notion of it happening to us at any time hadn't crossed our minds. We must have had some really good angels on guard, because we continued to do this so often, and we were never struck by lightning. We owe a big thanks to God.

A Day of Reckoning

Penny and I were not so involved in the learning process of maturity, but the forces of nature and peer pressure compelled us to be concerned about it. We didn't like the idea of physically maturing or becoming pansies very much, but we had no choice.

We learned a little bit about maturity in school from other girls that spoke and acted like "grown-ups." Sometimes the school had the health teacher give instruction about the miraculous, special process of becoming a woman. Or we did the smart thing; we went to the library and got information there or asked sisters. The expressions on their faces when we approached them with the questions we asked! They were really a great support to our maturity. I do believe they were so supportive of us because they were so worried for us. We also had some personal trainers, my brothers. They made sure we knew what not to do when we matured. They also drilled us on expectations that many guys may have.

As we began to mature we learned and became cautious about boys. For quite a long time we believed that holding hands with a boy was bad because it could lead to kissing, and kissing could cause pregnancy. Taking a sip out of the straw from a pregnant woman was also a no-no.

One nice, hot, summer day we decided to go swimming. We wanted to go, especially because we had both bought ourselves a blue, two-piece bathing suit that were almost alike, except that Penny's had a ruffle across her fanny. (This was one of those girl things we did). We just knew we were going to be a big hit! Well, our bubbles burst while we were showering before we went into the pool. A couple of girls our age that had the bodies of seventeen year-olds teased us. They told us we looked "cute," and weren't we embarrassed to be so flat chested and skinny.

"I would wear a T-shirt if I were you."

Our first thought was to clobber the heck out of them, but that would only prove we took their insults to heart; also, we would have been tossed out of the pool and we didn't want that. We enjoyed our time at the pool.

After that, we were reluctant to go out into the pool area because we were so embarrassed, though we quickly brushed it ff. Before stepping out, we peeked to see who was there, and to make sure we weren't being watched. The water in the pool was a nice, cool, sparkling color. There was absolutely no way embarrassment was keeping us out, we were so ready to jump in and refresh ourselves from the heat.

At one end of the pool, near the diving area, were the high school kids that were able to swim better, with a few younger kids that would sneak in, only to be removed by the lifeguards. In the five and six-foot area were two boys that we had an attraction to (another girl thing). They were being occupied by those two sassy girls; of course they were flirting with them. Penny and I being the great and fearless swimmers that we were, usually hung around the three and four-foot area. Before we entered the pool, we reminded ourselves of the dangers that we could involve ourselves with if we were to show our femininity to those guys. I think it was a disappointment more than anything else. Se we decided to stay away from them.

We then pranced to the pool quickly, and jumped in. The water felt relaxing, and refreshing. We began to move around in the water, simulating good swimmers. In the middle of "backstroke" we were both tugged down into the water. Our first reaction was to clobber whoever dunked us in, but as we came out of the water and saw it was those two guys, we calmed down quickly, and slowly forgot all about being so careful around

boys. It was easier to do so since our brothers weren't around. We were surprised since they had been so preoccupied before. However, the biggest and best surprise was that they spent the rest of the swimming session with us. Maybe it was the bikinis, or our fantastic looks, or us in general; either way our burst bubbles were re-inflated, double!

Several of our escapades stand out in my mind, but I chose this one because as I think about it, it is hilarious, and like most of the things that we did…. Pretty dumb.
I'll call this:

Creepy Crawlers

My mom and dad had to take a trip to Tucson, Arizona, and they took my younger brothers and sisters with them. I don't recall where Mimmee was at the time, and Billy and Bobby had both left town as well, to different locations. My sisters were in their own homes, so Penny and I were all alone. We felt so grown-up. On our grown-up day we decide to make ourselves supper at my house, go into my room and listen to some music, and chat, mainly about boys; we also compared breast size/ A little later we became bored so we decided to count vehicles going by. Our street had its share of traffic. We began: a car went by, we marked it; a truck, a motorcycle, a cop, etc. While sitting on the bed near the windowsill, we heard something outside, near the other window;

It sounded like footsteps. We continued with our great pastime. When we heard the sound again, we both turned to look at one another with fear.

"What was that!" Penny exclaimed.

"I don't know, it's probably Hot Dog." I replied.

So together we crept to the window to take a look. We saw the dog lying down without a care in the world. So we thought it was probably just the wind, the house settling, or whatever. We relaxed when again, we heard footsteps and a scratch on the window screen in my mom and dad's room. We then decided, It's Billy, or Bobby, they're back early, they're trying to frighten us.

"They're doing a good job," whispered Penny.

We got brave and called out for them both; no answer.

We then yelled out, "If you guys re trying to scare us, it's not working!" Yeah, right!

"We're gonna tell my mom and dad if you don't cut it out!" But no one responded We then heard a sound as if someone was trying to pull the screen off the bathroom window.

Remembering that we lived right across the street from the police station, and prisoners are kept there, and there have been prisoners that have escaped, several things went through our minds. What if there is an escaped prisoner outside? What if he is trying to kill us? He'll probably assault us! But why isn't the dog barking? He's probably dead by now, we thought.

Then we really began to panic! Why hadn't anyone in the police station notified us about an escaped prisoner the way they had done before?

"We're gonna die," said Penny, full of fear and out of breath.

"No weren't not," I told her. "We'll have to defend ourselves. Let's go down on the floor and crawl to the kitchen. We'll get something from the cabinets and use them to hit the guy." "OK" barely came out of Penny. Never did it cross our simple minds that we could call the police, and they would be there in a matter of seconds. So on we crawled. I felt like a creepy crawler, but we thought we had a creepy crawler outside trying to kill us.

I turned to look at Penny and said, "We're gonna die, you're so white he's going to see us because you reflect!"

"Shut up!" she blasted at me. On we crept. We finally reached the kitchen and I opened one of the cabinet doors and got a cast iron pan, then I stood up on the side of the door behind the trash can. Penny stood behind the door. "Penny," I said quietly, " when he tries to come in we'll both hit him, OK?"

"OK," she said.

"What are you using to hit him with?" I asked her.

She then showed me a ladle.

"Are you crazy, what do you expect to do, feed him?"

"I'll hit his face," she said.

A few seconds later we heard something right near the door. Now, our door being an old-fashioned screen door with a latch lock, it was easy to get into, especially since my brothers had made a hole in the screen in order to unlatch to latch. So, there we stood. I peeked at the door and saw a finger unlatching the lock.

My heart fluttered up and down my body at least a thousand times in one second.

My mouth was extremely dry. I looked over at Penny. She looked even whiter than normal. I'm certain we weren't breathing. I raised the pan in a baseball position. I saw a person coming in. In the middle of my swing, and Penny's attack with her deadly spoon we heard..... "Terry, Penny, stop!!!"

It was Bobby. I stopped my swing about three-quarters of the way. I missed hitting him by inches. "What are you doing here, and what are you doing?" we blasted him with a thousand questions.

He simply said, "I wanted to scare you guys, but after a while I thought it wasn't working, so I thought I'd let myself in."

"You idiot, I could have killed you!"

Apparently, his truck had broken down on the way to his destination, so he'd had to return. After we had gathered our insides back together, we sat down to watch television.

We were nicely settled in when Bobby asked, "So, which one of you has the bigger breasts?"

An Eventful Day

Riding bikes was one of our favorite pastimes. Sometimes we rode on one bike; one of us would drive the bike and the other would sit on the handlebars. This is what we called pumping.

It was a nice spring day, so we decided to go for a cruise on my bike. Penny's bike was flat, so I pumped her. We cruised around a few blocks here and there. When we came back home, we began to kid around and pretended and to be stunt drivers. There we were, going up and down the three foot, slanted, sidewalk in front of the empty house, next door to my house. Sometimes I'd lose my balance and go another direction. Poor bike, poor Penny's behind. It must have hurt coming off the curb. She didn't complain, though. We continued. However, we were interrupted a couple of times by our parents sending us on errands and such. Then some people came by asking directions. We gave them directions as accurately as we could. Little did they know we weren't very good at giving directions. Finally, we were able to enjoy what we were doing. We were getting braver and braver, so we tried different tricks. The last stunt we did was a screamer, and biffed it!

Her we go, we went about a half block away from the sidewalk in order to gain speed. By the time we reached the sidewalk slant, we were going so fast that we lost control of the bike; up we go! I do believe we even flew for a few seconds. We turned as quickly as we could to avoid hitting the house. Around we went, and down the curb— bonk, bonk was the sound the bike made when we came off the curb.

Penny was hanging on for dear life, with a few screams in between bumps and hops, here braids flying every which way, even slapping my face a couple of times. Still out of control, we made a quick turn towards the library, but we were still going so fast that it was pretty difficult to slow down, much less stop. I noticed we were coming to the curb near the library,, so I hit the brakes. Suddenly, we crashed into the curb. Everything happened so quickly. The back of the bike came up from behind me. I held on to the handlebars and Penny was thrown forward off the bike. She literally flew over the concrete library fence and landed on the other side, on the grass! I let loose of the bike and ran over to see if Penny had survived the fall.

I was so scared, "Penny!" I frantically called out.

I looked over to the other side of the fence, where Penny was lying face down on the grass, arms and legs spread out about her.

"Are you OK?"

She turns herself around and says, "Yes, but we're fixing my bike!"

Scraped, bruised and bumped around, we walked to her backyard to get her bike fixed. Not even injuries scared us away from riding. After we fixed the flat tire, off we went again. We usually bought Sixlets candies but the two-for-a-penny candy would give us more, so, we chose those.

George, one of the owners of the REC hall, knew exactly what we went in for, even before we asked for it. We did this occasionally, we got our candies and took off.

It was my turn, the chain to my bike came loose (I wonder why?), so we stopped to fix it. The annoying thing was that it kept coming loose. We came around the corner of Eighth Street and Penn when a big white dog came out of nowhere! It was barking and growling at us as though we looked like its dinner. Penny, with those long legs, pedaled off quickly.

"Stop!" I yelled at her. "If you don't move it won't bite you."

She didn't bother listening to me and kept going. I would have kept going also, but I had no choice, the chain on my bike had come loose again. I stopped and the dog came at me. I knew I was dead meat!

I looked it straight in the eye and said, "Please don't bite me, dog!" The dog stopped growling and stared at me as though I was either crazy or just plain dumb. It must have felt sorry for me because it then gave me a soft bark, turned, and pranced off. I fixed the chain, again, and rode on. Penny was waiting for me one block away. As I reached her, I declared that bike riding for the day was over.

We went home, put the bicycles away, climbed in her mom and dad's little green car, and pretended to be driving. We pretended to run into certain friends while driving through the Dairy Queen just to show off. We quickly became bored and proceeded to my house. It wasn't very often we did this, but we made an exception today: we played "house" Rudy and Eddie were our husbands. Eddie was my husband, we called him Paul, after Paul McCartney.

Rudy was Penny's husband, we called him David, after David Cassidy. Mimee was Penny's baby, and I used a doll. Of course in these marriages, Penny and I made the rules.

A family had recently moved in next door to a house that Mr. and Mrs. Dimas rented next door to Penny's home. The woman in this family was a nurse, and she was what we called, a "snob." She made sure we knew we were dirty and full of germs. They had a daughter, and she was the same as her mother. Penny could not stand her. Since the first day we met her she tried to make our lives miserable. She was a constant nag and crybaby, and sarcastic to the max. This girl was a big girl, Penny and I together made one of her. Well, while we were playing house, here she come strolling to my back yard. We tried to be nice to her (my dad had to remind us), but this was one day Penny could no longer take her sarcasm. My mom had called me inside to take care of something, more than likely one of my nephews or nieces needed to be tended to. On my way outside I heard a ruckus. It was the kids trying to get Penny off of Sarah. Apparently Sarah had mouthed off one too many ties. Her insults were too much to have to put up with. Penny told her to be quiet. She didn't, so skinny Penny grabbed a hold of her, picked her up, and tossed her on the ground, then proceeded in clobbering her!

When we finally got Penny off of her, Sarah ran home, beaten. We were so glad that she had left, but at the same time we knew we were in trouble. But with the day we had already had, we didn't care much. So we stopped playing house sat on the swinging bench in the back yard, and waited for punishment. What a day! We had to wait all evening, but it finally came.

The day ended on a couple of good notes. First, we were allowed to stay up that night to watch television and eat burritos. Second, before my dad left to work he gave us a short lecture and our punishment. Which wasn't so severe for as big a fuss as her mother had made. We were punished from, get this, bike riding for a week, and we were not allowed to even look at Sarah which, frankly, suited us just fine. Third, my dad informed us that Sarah's family was moving in a month. Oh Joy, rapture, we thought to ourselves. So, for the remaining time that they were in town we obeyed the punishment given to us, and didn't look at crybaby Sarah, and she didn't come messing with us anymore. Especially not Penny!

Just for Fun and Need

For as much fun as we had there were days in our lives that were difficult. But we always stuck together, such as the times we could have gotten lost in the forest, or when we were ill.

My family was raised outdoors, and we used to go to the forest and rivers quite often. My mom would pack a lunch, my dad would get the gear ready. We enjoyed the outdoors very much! In the forest we would camp out, gather acorns, sometimes berries, or *nopales* (cactus). My dad would teach us about the forest, getting around in it, about the animals, what to do, and what not to do. We would also play games, or just run down the mountains. We would normally arrive back home with a few bumps and bruises, but never anything serious. Penny and I, adventurers that we were, would gout walking in the woods (looking for bears). We saw other animals, but we never did find a bear. Good thing, I am not sure what we would have done if we had found one.

There were a couple of times on our way back to the camp area when we believed we were lost. Of course, we became a bit frightened, but we always got our bearings back on track, and we would get back safely. As we were getting near the camp, we heard our names being called. We knew we were in trouble! We would get scolded up on our arrival, and we would try to explain our whereabouts and give assurance that we were fine. But needless to say, we were still punished. Naturally, they were all glad to have us back sage and sound. We were teased all the way home, by—guess who—of course, our brothers. Even during the teasing we enjoyed the ride home. We would have a snack or two, something to drink, and we would get to listen to music. Sometimes Spanish, or our groovy rock music. Many times we all sand. We weren't lost and we didn't get eaten by a bear, although, believe it or not, we really wanted to find one. It wasn't so bad; we were together.

On days we did not have so much to do we would make something up. Sometimes we would get a June bug and tie its legs to a string. It would fly around and around. It sounded like a blimp flying overhead, or a swarm of bees. It was just a way to pass the time and have some fun. Other times we would sing and dance. One evening, along with Rudy, Eddie, Penny and Mimee, we were in my room playing games and singing. Anita was in a fussy mood that day; she seemed to want to get anyone in trouble. She would come in to the room and disturb, or pick on us, then run to the living room where my mom and dad were and tell on us, even if it wasn't true. I finally did do something to her; I smacked her butt! She ran inside to tell on me, but my dad had already had enough of her tattling. He scolded her and made her stay away from us.

Eddie had stepped out of the room for a short time while we were singing a great rendition of "Close to You" by the Carpenters. Penny was recording us with a small recorder. We were glad Anita was gone so we teased her. We recorded a benediction to her. It went like this; Penny said, "Let us share a few moments of silence for our dearly departed *piojo* (lice)." We bowed our heads in silence, when suddenly, Eddie came in with a lit match, burning his fingers, screaming, "Fire, Fire!" I t disrupted our sincere moment, but we all laughed. Anita pouted and my Dad scolded us, disallowing us from using the recorder for the rest of the day. Eddie was also punished for playing with matches. Anita still had to remain away from us so she watched us from the door. To this day Penny still has that recording.

A day or two later, Penny came over and said, "We're moving!" That was tragic! What were we going to do, how could we be apart? How could her parents do that to us! We decided to check out the house that Mr. and Mrs. Dimas intended to buy. It was a nice house, only it was four or five blocks away from my house! We found several reasons why they shouldn't buy it. We spoke to Mrs. Dimas daily and asked her questions about moving. We also put in our two, or ten, cents as to why they shouldn't move. Inconspicuously, of course. It was greatly bothering us; and our appetites were affected. Instead of eating our usual two or three servings, plus snacks in between every meal, we ate one serving, and maybe shared a snack, we were honestly disturbed about this, and there was nothing we could do. This continued on for a few weeks until Mr. and Mrs. Dimas announced their plans had changed. So filled with joy, we could eat again; we were relieved! Naturally, we believed we had made a difference in their decision.

For some time, I had a problem with a rash that was all over my body. At first, it was only on my arms, then it spread. I was taken to several doctors, but they were unable to help. It was making me hurt badly, and interfering in our daily lives. A doctor was afraid I might have leprosy! How in the world could I catch leprosy? My dad asked the Dr. He pretty much let that Dr. know what he thought of his diagnosis, and, of him! My parents were worried about this, and the fact no one seemed to be able to cure it. They searched for doctors left and right until finally my sister-in-law Martha came across a friend that recommended a Dr. This Dr. saved me. He found the problem and knew the cure. When I arrived at home, Penny had picked up my homework for me, and she also helped me with my chores because I was limited on what I could do. On the day we arrived from doctors with the cure we began the treatment. I had to wash the affected areas and apply medicine. I began to wash up softly when Penny came in and reminded me the doctor wanted me to wipe, not dab. So she took the paper towel I had to use from me and proceeded to wash me. I thought I was going to die, it hurt! I screamed with agony, and Penny would tell me not to move, and this is how we have to do it. So she did it, I believe she enjoyed making me suffer. Though, that really was the way it was supposed to be done. Then she applied the ointment. Not once did she ever cringe or turn away from me when I had that problem. She helped me get well. It took a while for me to get back to normal, but eventually I did. That was one of the worst times of my life. I was delighted to be able to do the normal, everyday things we normally take for granted. This brought us to thinking seriously, for once.

Some time later we began thinking about dying, getting lost or moving, and we felt we should do something in order for us never to be apart from one another. We were in my room pondering how we could possibly remain together for the rest of our lives. After some long, careful, consideration, we came up with the solution. We decided to become blood sisters. Sisters are never apart, you know; blood is thicker than separation. We got one of my dad's twist-off razor blades from his shaver and proceeded with our sisterly transformation. We slightly cut our thumbs with the razor from the shaver. Penny cut hers first. She let out such a painful scream that I almost chickened out after seeing that it hurt. I finally did it, before Penny bled to death. We put our thumbs together and held them that way for a while. Magic took place. We just knew it worked; we became blood sisters. We wrapped our thumbs with a sock when suddenly my dad knocked on the door. He opened the door and asked, "What are you doing?"

"Nothing, just playing," we said while holding our hands behind us.

"Behave," he said.

"We will," we replied. He closed the door and we breathed a sigh of relief. We were thrilled, but in some pain. That didn't matter to us; we would always be together now!

During all the years we lived across the street from one another, we rarely spent time apart. Not even when we were going through growing stages. We now live in the same city, a few blocks apart. We have our own families, and to this day we still remain the best of friends. If I had to have chosen a friend for myself before our existence, I would have chosen one just like her. There is no better one for me, and we're blood sisters to top it off!